GW00630580

Humility

A Reflection for Social Leaders

Design & Typesetting by: SWATT Books Ltd.

Printed in the United Kingdom
First Printing, 2021

ISBN: 978-1-8380196-4-8 (Hardback)
ISBN: 978-1-8380196-5-5 (eBook)

Sea Salt Learning
www.julianstodd.wordpress.com
www.seasaltlearning.com

Contents

On Humility

These pages form a reflection on humility and how, in the Social Age, leadership may need to be more 'humble' than 'heroic'.

My work explores the context of the Social Age, and the ways that we must adapt, as societies, within organisations, and as individual leaders: it considers a deep seated need for fairness in all that we do, and the social accountability of those who fail to act so.

This reflective essay forms part of that journey: it considers whether, and how, we can learn to be more humble and fair as Social Leaders[1].

It is intended neither as a definition of humility nor a route map to get you there.

If anything, it's an individual reflection.

My own reflection, and structured as such. My own understanding and truth.

At best, I hope it provides you with a set of thoughts to kick off from: a place to start. But I should warn you that I suspect humility itself is not a destination, but rather a measure of, and judgement upon, the journey that we take.

Your truth is yours to find.

I know people who are humble, but few who would describe themselves as such. The badge of humility may be one that is bestowed.

With that thought, humility may not be a state that we attain, but is, perhaps, a light that is shone upon our actions.

It's not an intention, but rather a judgement. A measurement upon, or a shadow of, our deeds.

This Book

This book is the shortest book I have written, and may be the shortest book you will ever read.

It is spaced out: you can cross out those lines that anger you, or add in the words that have meaning for you.

If you enjoy it, you can treasure it,
or gift it onwards, graffiti and all.

You may read it from the front, or dip in, to pull one line or page from the centre.

If something resonates with you: consider sharing it. Ask a question, or find a conversation, to explore it in company.

Winning

Gain is not a finite resource: we can all win.

Your success does not deplete mine. Sharing can empower us both.

These pages are a commentary about winning, but strangely, winning by giving everything away.

Where I have found financial success and security, I have found that comfort, belonging, and meaning do not accompany it: by contrast, where I have shared experience, challenge, hardship, or pain, I have left with greater wealth than money can represent.

It is not always a question of how you win, but rather where you win, and what you have won.

And sometimes, whether the price was worth paying.

Society

We have constructed our society: it's an aggregated, shared belief system. It is a common and consensual delusion.

A made-up collection of stories.

Our social norms, each with a history, are often contested, and all, subject to our whim, are able to change. If we choose to rewrite them. Or if a new narrative is imposed upon us.

Take equality. Society has constantly moved, adapted, evolved, not fast enough for some, yet too fast for others.

Change has happened through consensus, and through opposition.

Change has often been framed by bold action and sacrifice, and led through brave leadership.

But change is not simply about the loud and visible. It's about our individual actions in the moment.

Kindness, respect, gentle reason.

Sharing, storytelling, story listening.

Brave leaders can be humble, but leaders are only one part of the system (unless we consider Social Leaders, who are the system).

I might reflect on how our aggregated normalisation of behaviours has left us in a difficult place: a world dominated by oppositional power, the partisanship of occluded, unequal, divisive politics, arguably played by the wealthy, for individual gain, more than by the many, for the good of society.

The professional and performance nature of politics today may have led it to simply form an extension of the market.

Regulator and beneficiary rolled into one. Those who win continue to win.

There are poor politicians, but they form a minority. It may take more effort for a politician to remain poor than to ride the waves of power and to accumulate wealth and yet more power.

Stop to consider how those who are more senior in a hierarchy are often wealthier: is that an innate state, a default law of nature, or a constructed and accepted truth?

The rich gain power and power gains riches.

Of course, humility is not about poverty. There is no reason that a rich woman may not be humble, and a poor man arrogant.

But when riches equate to status, is that fair?

Within industry, the market rewards success.

Success, it can seem, at all costs.

We may not seek the hero leader, but the financial reward, and the risk of failure, may drive us there.

Inherently it can seem as though the role of leadership is to direct, and the role of others is to follow.

Possibly the role of leaders is to gain, and the cost of followers to pay the bills.

But the corollary of this is not true: the strength, the win, does not come from pointing in the right direction.

True strength lies in carrying the load, and when that load is shared throughout the system.

The question to ask is not 'How much weight can you carry?', but rather 'How much, from your burden, can I relieve?'.

To carry heavy weights together.

The model whereby we pay the people at the top more money is, itself, a social construct.

Power systems based upon physical dominance have led to power systems based upon resource dominance, and hence into organisational structures based upon pure power dominance.

I have it: you lack it.

I win and hence you lose.

And because you have lost, you are worth less than me: the poor, the worker, the teacher, the kind man, the generous woman.

Worth less.

Worthless.

We rarely celebrate those who give everything away as much as those who sit upon a hoard.

The normalisation of behaviours, from politics to industry, leaves us here, in the 21st century, with a model that may be flawed.

Our hierarchies of power and wealth may be outdated. It may be that we need strength throughout our systems, not simply heroes at the top. And we may need more distributed fairness, not simply contractual bonds.

Broad fairness: a system that is fair, led with humility.

Perhaps we should seek to remake our society with humility: a society where kindness forms our basis for action, where pride often sits in the achievements of others, and where the greatest good comes from being a humble leader.

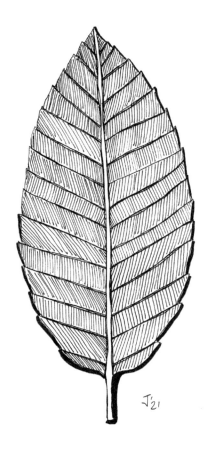

Salvation

The 21st century is feeling the impacts of collaborative technology, technology that can connect us globally, and yet reinforces our divisions. Technology that makes us better, and yet makes us worse.

A worse parody of ourselves. Fake news, institutional bias, revenge porn sites and trolling.

Technology will not make us humble.

Indeed, some would argue that most current paradigms of social media encourage egotism and narcissistic pride.

They reward the vain with 'likes'.

They are mechanisms of colour and blood: voyeuristic amplifications of titillation and muck.

Yet they are also mechanisms of hope and freedom.

This is our dilemma. Good and evil.

Technology will not save us, but it needn't damn us either. We already do that for ourselves.

Perhaps the humility we need is humility distributed throughout a system: a system that listens as much as it talks.

That gives respect as much as it demands attention.

The world sits on the edge of a precipice: deepening wealth inequality, ongoing resource depletion, widespread political turmoil, a climate crisis and the unsettling of the established order, gender-based power imbalances, failed national approaches to immigration, systemic racism and homophobia, insurgency, failed or failing financial models.

We see foundational shifts in organisations, forces at play that will transform everything: the potential (or threat) of automation, emergence of AI and machine learning permeating every aspect of decision making and control, imposed social accountability, the urgency of privacy, the rise of the transnationals, the fractured Social Contract that governs our relationship with institutional systems, democratised creativity and the consequences of failing to be deeply fair.

Our salvation will not come from our politicians and bankers, from our legal systems or bosses.

It won't be a solution imposed from above.

If we are to step back from the brink, it will be through a distributed, yet aggregated, salvation.

It will be quiet voices that will lead. It will be consensus and respect that drive the unity.

All of this will happen if we can find humility in leadership.

There will be no single hero, but rather the heroism of simplicity.

Leadership with kindness, unity through humility.

Salvation, if it comes from anywhere, may start within. It may start by asking questions:

Not 'What will you do?', but 'How can I listen?'

Not 'Who can I blame?', but 'How can I help?'

Not 'What will it cost?', but 'What am I prepared to invest?'

The answers may not come through hierarchical leadership, but rather distributed leadership. Social Leadership.

They may not come from bold steps from the front, but rather from quiet steps in every direction.

The leadership we need may be strong, but it will be humble.

This book is a reflection on humility in leadership: why humility may be the hardest thing to gain, and the easiest thing to fall by the wayside.

Writing about humility does not mean that one is humble: just the opposite in fact, it may be an aspiration for a journey, the start of a sketch map to travel through.

A map we all need to draw.

Listening

We easily spend the time we should be listening, deciding what to say instead.

The pace, the tempo, the demands, of our everyday encourage a response more so than silence.

We seek to validate, to deny, to counter, or respond, to any story that is shared: outside of a music gig or theatre performance, we rarely find a pure space to listen, and permission to do just that.

We are conditioned to add our voice.

Silence is not affirmation.

Silence can be respectful.

Silence can be a breath, a pause or a deeper moment of contemplation.

Silence can be the wave that washes the sand clean again.

We can listen: feel ourselves connect in anger, or denial, in pride or with power, but let that wash away, move into reflection and consideration: move into acceptance and gratitude.

Humility may be to find ourself by listening more so than speaking.

To find ourself in community more so than upon a plinth.

To find ourself in reflection more so than a hasty answer.

To find ourself in our ability to listen, then change, more so than to listen and then shout.

Roots

Where are you grounded?

Our roots form the foundation of our power: we may be grounded within a system, a structure, a formal framework.

Our roots may be our qualifications, our rank, our seniority, our wealth, our status or our job title.

Roots hold us steady, but they hold us still.

Our roots make us safe, whilst holding us true to systems that may be outdated.

Our roots may indenture us to power.

Roots can make it hard to change.

Humility may be the process of unhitching ourselves from status within a system and investing ourselves, instead, in service of the people around us.

If humility gives us power, it is a power that is granted, not claimed.

To be humble in our approach is not to forgo power or opportunity, but perhaps, instead, to open ourselves up to a new form of power.

To be considered, to be reflective, to be generous, to be thoughtful – these are things that come at no cost.

We can be reflective, yet still decisive.

We can be generous with our encouragement, our gratitude, and our connections: generosity does not require money.

Wisdom is our notion of the considered response: to be a wise woman, or a wise man, brings images of grey hair and wrinkled smiles, but wisdom does not need to be scholarly and purely a feature of age.

We can have 'wisdom beyond our years', as though it were an exception.

Perhaps to be a child is, itself, a form of humility, for we have not yet learned to be constrained, or arrogant, in full measure.

We start unmade, then make ourselves less.

Homelessness

When I walk past someone begging in the street, I imagine an imposed humility: the roles that one can play in this tenuous situation are limited.

> *Losing a home is to lose status and value in a modern society.*

'Of no fixed abode' is a fancy way of saying 'of little value'.

Again, we equate the value of a life to the wealth and status that accompanies it.

We call out 'aggressive' begging as though it were an affront, but one may ask what is wrong with the demand that is made?

Is the default state we seek to all be equal, or should our society be inherently differentiated by power and wealth?

Humble and poor, or possibly cheeky and chirpy: these are the choices faced by those who are homeless.

Aggression may be an option, but with higher consequences.

To demand is not seen as humility: rather we prefer to see our response to homelessness as charity and magnanimity, as opposed to fairness and duty.

That correlation between poverty and humility is hard to escape.

For the beggar, humility may be imposed, whilst for the rich, it could be a luxury that we can choose to afford.

I'm not sure how comfortable that makes me, or, perhaps more importantly, what I should do with that discomfort.

The relevance of homelessness to leadership is the way it allows us to consider both the edges of our social systems, as well as the connection between status and value.

And to ask ourselves if our actions have more value when they are seen, or when they are carried in small moments of kindness that are never witnessed.

Which may be a question of whether the good that we do is valuable in itself, or simply when it is witnessed and judged by others.

Pride

We may feel pride in our own achievements, or in those of others.

Is pride a counterpoint to humility? Is it OK to be proud as a measurement of one's actions, but still humble in word and deed?

Is humility simply internal, or can it be worn as a measure on one's sleeve?

I find pride in the achievements of others, and am not alone in this: when I see my friends succeed, when I see their strength and humility, it makes me proud, so pride itself surely does not detract from humility.

Or, perhaps, it does so when one feels it about oneself?

> *A humble person may be proud of others, but to be prideful of oneself may erode that trait.*

I'm not sure: when I think of my friends, I can think of people who are both humble and proud.

It's easier to see this in others.

Perhaps it's a matter of degree, or a matter of internalisation versus external projection?

One can feel quiet pride, with humility, but one must not be boastful: is this an overexertion of pride?

Surely the humble leader can be proud too?

Not only of others, but of themselves and their achievements?

What is the relationship between pride and humility?

The Humble Leader

Take a moment to consider yourself as a leader.

The only thing we can truly change is ourselves, but to change ourselves carries great power. It's just one step to lead from the 'back' to the 'front'.

Our actions form a story.

Whilst we control our part within it, we do not control the way it lands.

Others will read it, but it will be for them to judge it.

And then they will write our story upon us.

I picked up a book yesterday, the last book written by one of my favourite authors before his early death.

The cover had his name in a silver foil embossed upon it.

When I put the book down, traces of silver remained stuck to my fingers.

I smiled at the irony: his ideas remain in my mind, shaping and influencing my thoughts, and even the book cover was reaching out, literally spreading itself.

How will people look upon your story?

What will they take away when they hear you, when you touch their lives?

When one of my friends was bullied at work, a leader said he 'stood alongside her'.

But I did not care where he stood, because in his act of standing, he failed to speak out.

He sympathised, but through silence condoned the wrongdoing.

Our words form colour, but the hard edge is our actions.

Our thoughts may rationalise, but sometimes the white heat of action comes from words.

Brave words.

Sometimes change must be talked for, and sometimes fought for.

And there is always a price. So what price are you willing to pay?

Words change everything, from the softest whisper to the loudest shout.

Cries of hope or pain.

How will your words touch the world?

How will you listen to the words of others?

Will you be known for the picture of strength that you project, or for the shadow that you cast in your wake?

Being a humble leader may require bold action, but action not for self, but for others.

Words spoken not in vanity, but generosity.

Actions taken in service of others, not to take more for ourselves.

Our humble leadership is a reflection, a journey.

Consider the traces of your actions, the faint sketch outline of the map that you make as you travel.

Consider your journey, and do not defer the hardest steps for tomorrow, or for others to take.

Step forward to be a humble leader, and then carry others so that they can pass you.

Not in idealism and fantasy, but in humility and kindness, with generosity and respect.

Social leaders do not just look up with ambition, but down with humility.

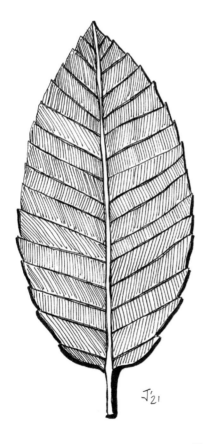

Reflection

I wanted to write this as a reflective essay: a poem almost, a reflection upon humility.

My fear lies in trite aphorisms and hollow words.

But we must make space for these conversations.

It's OK to talk about humility, because we have to make a change.

We live in a world largely predicated on what I can take, and the cost that I can defer.

But this cannot last.

We need a world where we can collaborate, where we can find respect, where humility drives our actions.

And if we build that world, we will lose nothing: not riches, status, power or pride.

Because everything that counts lies in our shadow, the shadow we cast upon the world. And the thing about the shadow is that you cannot see into it: we rely on others to help us find our way.

Perhaps ultimately humility will prove to be a collective phenomena?

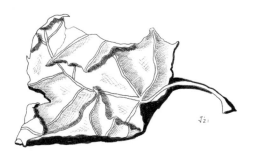

This book

The leaves of this book represent us all, blown by the winds of our everyday lives.

It is as we are buffeted and blown that we cast our shadow.

Like the best exercise plan, it's easy to visualise our better selves tomorrow, but we can instead be our better selves today.

Where you see injustice, fight it.

Where you see others stand firm, stand alongside them.

Where people shout, whisper in kindness.

Where people are lost, help them find hope.

When things are wrong, make them right, and don't compromise for short term gain, because money means nothing if it costs us our humanity. Or our humility.

When you have everything, think of those without.

If you have nothing, share your kindness.

Our impact runs through our journey: it's your journey to shape.

About Julian Stodd

Author

Artist

Reader

Explorer

Occasional thinker

Frequently wrong

www.julianstodd.wordpress.com

@julianstodd

www.SeaSaltLearning.com

Endnotes

1   Formal leaders gain their power from their position within a hierarchy: Social Leaders, by contrast, earn their authority through their actions within their Communities. My book, 'The Social Leadership Handbook' provides a detailed overview of this from an individual perspective. My most recent book on 'The Socially Dynamic Organisation' explores this in terms of Organisational Design.